SCHOLARS OF SCIENCE

ROB COLSON

CRABTREE
PUBLISHING COMPANY
WWW.CRABTREEBOOKS.COM

Pioneers in science, technology, engineering, and math

Published in Canada
Crabtree Publishing
616 Welland Avenue
St. Catharines, ON
L2M 5V6

Published in the United States
Crabtree Publishing
PMB 59051
350 Fifth Ave, 59th Floor
New York, NY 10118

Published in 2019 by Crabtree Publishing Company

First Published in Great Britain in 2018 by Wayland
Copyright © Hodder and Stoughton, 2018

Author: Rob Colson

Editorial director: Kathy Middleton

Editors: Elise Short, Crystal Sikkens

Proofreader: Ellen Rodger

Designer: Ben Ruocco

Prepress technician: Ken Wright

Print coordinator: Katherine Berti

The website addresses (URLs) included in this book were valid at the time of going to press. However, it is possible that contents or addresses may have changed since the publication of this book. No responsibility for any such changes can be accepted by either the author or the Publisher.

Images:
t–top, b–bottom, l–left, r–right, c–center,
front cover–fc, back cover–bc
All images courtesy of Dreamstime.com and all icons made by Freepik from www.flaticon.com, unless indicated:

Inside front Jubalharshaw19; fc, bc Deviney; fcr, 26-27 Hamster3d; fcbl, 6-7 Silverstore; 3t Igor Netkov; 4cl Ludovisi Collection; 4-5 Jrabelo; 5cr CERN; 5 Bryljaev; 7c Stockerteam; 7br Fat*fa*tin; 8l Georgios; 8-9 NASA; 12l Potysiev Denis; 13tr Choreograph; 14-15 Overcrew55; 15b, 23br Smashicons; 16-17 Soeten; 17 br Vectors Market; 18br CTBTO; 19bl, 21cr Roundicons; 20-21 NASA/ESA; 23tr NASA / WMAP Science Team; 24b Klikk; 25t Designua; 27tr Franklin and Gosling; 28bl ShareAlike 2.5 Generic (CC BY-SA 2.5); 29b Leocalvett; 31cl Adogslifephoto; 31cr Jfspic; 31cr Scanrail.

Every effort has been made to acknowledge every image source but the publisher apologises for any unintentional errors or omissions that will be corrected in future editions of this book.

Printed in the U.S.A./122018/CG20181005

Library and Archives Canada Cataloguing in Publication

Colson, Rob, 1971-, author
          Scholars of science / Rob Colson.

(STEM-gineers)
Includes index.
Issued in print and electronic formats.
ISBN 978-0-7787-5738-2 (hardcover).--
ISBN 978-0-7787-5824-2 (softcover).--
ISBN 978-1-4271-2235-3 (HTML)

          1. Science--History--Juvenile literature. 2. Discoveries in science--Juvenile literature. 3. Scientists--Biography--Juvenile literature. I. Title.

Q126.4.C66 2018   j509   C2018-905456-5
                                                                        C2018-905457-3

Library of Congress Cataloging-in-Publication Data

Names: Colson, Rob, 1971- author.
Title: Scholars of science / Rob Colson.
Description: New York, New York : Crabtree Publishing Company, 2019. | Series: STEM-gineers | "First published in Great Britain in 2018 by Wayland." | Includes index.
Identifiers: LCCN 2018043639 (print) | LCCN 2018045314 (ebook) | ISBN 9781427122353 (Electronic) | ISBN 9780778757382 (hardcover) | ISBN 9780778758242 (pbk.)
Subjects: LCSH: Science--History--Juvenile literature. | Discoveries in science--Juvenile literature. | Scientists--Biography--Juvenile literature.
Classification: LCC Q126.4 (ebook) | LCC Q126.4 .C655 2019 (print) | DDC 509--dc23
LC record available at https://lccn.loc.gov/2018043639

CONTENTS

SEEKING SCIENTIFIC KNOWLEDGE

Scientists seek knowledge about the world around us. To do this, they make careful observations, which lead to new **theories**. Scientists design experiments to test their theories. Depending on the evidence of the experiments, good theories are kept and bad ones are discarded.

Scientists in ancient times

Early scientists often worked in many different areas of knowledge. One of the first scientists, the ancient Greek, Aristotle (384–322 BCE), wrote about physics, biology, astronomy, and psychology. Today, scientists usually specialize in one field of study.

Building knowledge

Scientists make new discoveries by building on the work of the scientists that came before them. In this way, our scientific knowledge grows. When asked to describe his own discoveries in 1675, the famous English **physicist** Isaac Newton paid respect to other scientists by saying, "If I have seen further it is only by standing on the shoulders of giants."

The scientific method

The scientific method is a process that scientists follow in order to increase their understanding of a problem. The scientific method usually consists of these steps:

1. **Ask a question.**

2. **Carry out research by gathering information and making observations.**

3. **Make a hypothesis, which is a guess about what the answer might be.**

4. **Design an experiment to test your hypothesis, making a prediction of what will happen.**

5. **Analyze your results and present your conclusion.**

Using this method, scientists are able to collect evidence that supports their theories. They can also use the scientific method to show that a theory is wrong.

Scientists in the Islamic world were among the first to use the scientific method more than 1,000 years ago. In the 800s, Persian **chemist**, Jabir ibn Hayyan, was one of the first scientists to carry out experiments in a laboratory.

Teamwork

Scientists often work together in large teams. At the European Organization for Nuclear Research (CERN), thousands of scientists carry out experiments using the Large Hadron Collider. This machine smashes together tiny **subatomic particles** at close to the speed of light. This recreates conditions from near the beginning of the universe to test theories about the structure of space.

Read on to discover the challenges that scientists have overcome through the ages. The answers to each project's questions are found on page 31.

THE THEORY OF LIGHT

Light is a form of energy called electromagnetic radiation, which travels in the form of a wave. The scientific study of light is called optics. One of the first people to describe how light behaves was Arab **astronomer** and mathematician Ibn al-Haytham.

Ibn al-Haytham (about 965–1040 BCE)

Ibn al-Haytham worked in Cairo, Egypt, where he performed experiments using lenses and mirrors to show that light travels in straight lines. He also described the way that light is refracted, or bent, as it passes from air into water.

Bending light

Light moves at different speeds depending on the substance it must pass through. For example, light passes more slowly through water than it does through air. These differing speeds cause a beam of light to appear to bend as it passes from air into water. This is called **refraction.** Refraction makes an object underwater appear to be closer to the surface than it really is. Seabirds learn to allow for refraction when they dive for fish. Otherwise, they would always miss their prey.

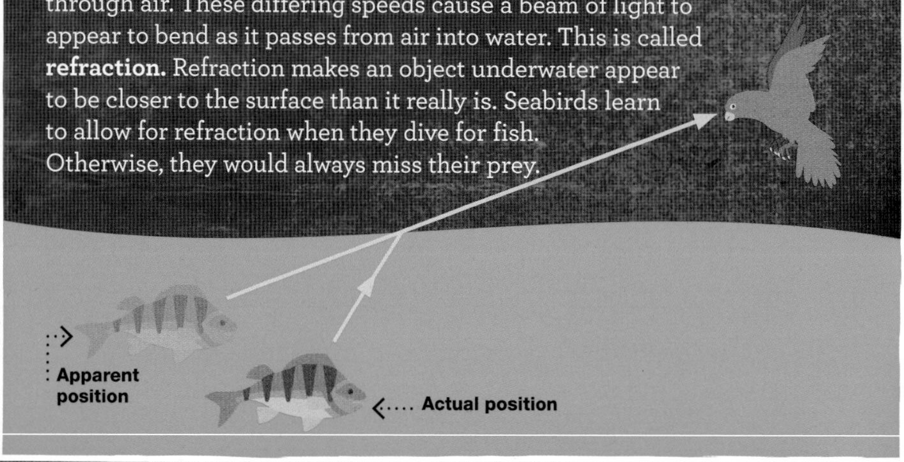

Apparent position

<···· Actual position

Splitting light

Ibn al-Haytham discovered that white light is made up of all the colors of the rainbow. A glass **prism** can separate the colors out by refraction. Each color is made by light waves with a particular wavelength. Wavelengths are measured in nanometers (nm). There are one billion nanometers in one meter (3.2 feet). For instance, red light has a wavelength of about 700 nm, while blue light has a wavelength of about 450 nm. Each wavelength is refracted by the prism at a slightly different angle, which splits the light into its separate colors.

Prism

Image on the eye

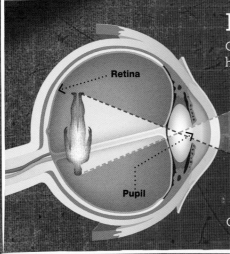

Retina

Pupil

Our eye captures light through a small hole at the front called the pupil. It forms an upside-down image on the lining of tissue at the back of the eye, called the retina. Light entering the pupil is refracted by the curve of the eyeball, turning the image upside-down. Our brains turn the image rightside up.

PROJECT:
CAMERA OBSCURA

A device called a camera obscura creates images much like those made by our eyes. This one is simple to make.

You will need: an empty cereal box and its empty inner bag, tape, a pin, scissors, and a source of light, such as a light bulb

1. Cut out a large rectangle from the front of the box and tape the inner bag over the hole to make a screen.

2. Use the pin to make a small hole in the side of the box that is opposite the screen.

3. Hold the pinhole-side of your camera obscura close to a light bulb, and see an image of the bulb appear on the screen.

Which way up is the image?

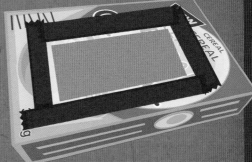

A UNIVERSAL FORCE

Gravity is a **force** that pulls all objects toward one another. The greater **mass** an object has, the greater its pull of gravity. Earth's gravitational pull is the force that gives us our weight. Without it, we would float off into space.

Isaac Newton (1643–1727)

English scientist Isaac Newton studied many different areas of science. Newton was the first person to realize that, not only is gravity the force that makes an apple fall from a tree, it is also what keeps Earth on a path circling the Sun.

Newton also used math to describe how the force of gravity gets weaker as the distance between objects increases. If you double the distance, you reduce the pull of gravity between objects to exactly one quarter of the strength.

Weight

Our own mass is a measure of the amount of matter, or material, we are made of. Mass is different than weight. Our weight is the strength of the force of gravity between us and Earth. Weight is measured using a unit called the newton (N). Our weight on other planets would be different from our weight on Earth since their gravitational pull is not the same.

Jupiter

Earth

Escape velocity

Newton imagined what would happen if a cannon fired a ball from a high mountain. At low speeds, the cannonball would fall to Earth, pulled by Earth's gravity (red and green arrows on the illustration). However, fired with enough velocity, the ball would be placed into orbit around Earth (blue arrow). Fired with an even greater velocity, the ball would fly off into space (yellow arrow). This happens at a velocity of 25,020 mph (40,266 kph), which is called escape velocity.

Pluto

Equal acceleration

In 1590, Italian scientist Galileo Galilei (1564–1642) dropped two spheres of different mass from the top of the Tower of Pisa. Both balls hit the ground at the same time, showing that objects fall at the same acceleration, or increasing speed, regardless of their mass.

Mars

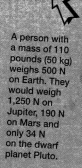

A person with a mass of 110 pounds (50 kg) weighs 500 N on Earth. They would weigh 1,250 N on Jupiter, 190 N on Mars and only 34 N on the dwarf planet Pluto.

PROJECT: BALL AND RAMP

Recreate Galileo's gravity experiment.

You will need: a pile of books, a piece of cardboard 3.2 feet (1 meter) long, a marble, and a stopwatch

1. Set up a ramp by resting one end of the cardboard on a stack of books. The books should be about 18 inches (40 cm) high to angle the ramp at about 30 degrees.

2. Measure a point a quarter of the distance from the top.

3. Roll a marble down the ramp. Use a stopwatch to time how long it takes to reach the quarter-point mark, and how long it takes to reach the bottom. Repeat four times. Take an average of your results by adding up all the quarter-point mark times and dividing by four. Do the same for the full-length times..

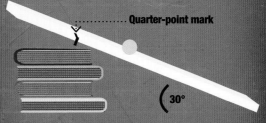

Quarter-point mark

30°

In your experiment, did the ball reach the quarter-point mark in about half the time it took to reach the bottom? Galileo discovered that falling objects accelerate at a constant rate. Mathematically, this means that the distance traveled increases by a square of the time.

THE ORIGIN OF SPECIES

In 1859, the English **naturalist** Charles Darwin published a book outlining a new theory explaining the origin, or source, of the different life-forms we see today, known as species.

❶ Large beak for cracking nuts

❸ Small beak for small seeds, fruit, and insects

Charles Darwin (1809–1882)

Darwin's new idea, called evolution, was that new species of life appear over long periods of gradual change. This change is caused by a process he called natural selection, in which species that adapt best to their habitats pass on their own strong characteristics, or **traits**, to their offspring, or children. In this way, species change, or evolve, over time.

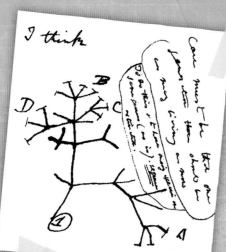

Darwin spent many years developing his theory, which was highly controversial at the time. Today, scientists have collected huge amounts of evidence to support his theory, which is one of the most powerful ideas in science.

Darwin made these drawings of four species of finches he observed on the Galápagos Islands.

In 1837, still unsure of his theory, Darwin drew this "Tree of Life" in his notebook to show how species are related. He wrote "I think" above it.

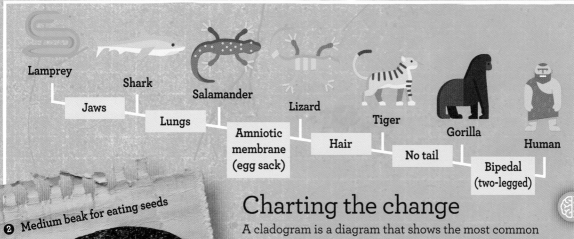

Charting the change

A cladogram is a diagram that shows the most common ancestor of different species. This cladogram shows how humans are related to other species. Each species has all the traits to the left of its branch but none of the traits to the right. For example, the gorilla has no tail, has hair, an egg sack, lungs, and jaws, but it is not two-legged.

2 Medium beak for eating seeds

4 Thin beak for catching insects

Darwin's finches

While visiting the Galápagos Islands in the Pacific Ocean, Darwin noticed that finches on different islands had differently shaped beaks, depending on what food they ate. He believed that these finches were all descended from, or were related to, one species, known as a common ancestor. They became isolated on their islands and they could not mix together. New species with different beaks had evolved on each island, adapting to the different foods available to each of them.

PROJECT: EVOLUTION GAME

Evolution telephone is a game that you can play with a classroom of students or a group of friends.

> There are many strange species in the room today.

You will need: a group of friends

1. Players should sit or stand in a circle. The first person whispers a phrase into the ear of the person to their left, making sure nobody else hears.

2. The second person then whispers the phrase they heard to the next person and so on around the circle. Note how the phrase has changed by the time it returns to the first person.

> The cat said hello to everyone from its favorite corner.

Try to make the first phrase a strange-sounding one. This will make the changes more dramatic. The changes occur because a person mishears the phrase and repeats a different one. In evolution, a similar process happens. Changes called mutations occur when units called genes are miscopied during reproduction. These mutations are then passed on to a new generation. Many mutations are harmful, but some are useful. Useful mutations quickly spread.

> Everyone loves tuna and cheese, but never at the same table.

GERM THEORY OF DISEASE

For centuries, it was believed that infectious diseases that caused many deaths, such as cholera and the plague, were caused by a form of "bad air," called miasma. In the 1860s, French chemist Louis Pasteur showed how tiny **microbes**, called germs, were the actual cause.

Louis Pasteur
(1822–1895)

Pasteur aimed to disprove an old theory that life can appear from non-living matter. To do this, he came up with experiments that showed there were tiny invisible microbes, or germs, in the air. He also showed that certain microbes are the true cause of infectious diseases. This germ theory of disease was a major breakthrough in medical science.

Believing that the plague could be caught from "bad air," doctors in the Middle Ages wore masks with beaks to protect them from breathing it in. They did not know that the disease was caused by microbes so small that the beaks offered little protection.

The swan neck experiment

In one of his experiments, Pasteur prepared a rich broth, which he boiled to kill any microbes it might contain. He placed the broth in a flask, and attached a tube shaped like a swan's neck to it. The shape allowed air in, but trapped microbes in its bottom curve. The broth stayed uninfected. Then he broke the tube and allowed microbes to fall into the broth. The infected broth turned cloudy.

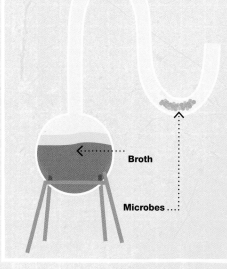

Broth

Microbes

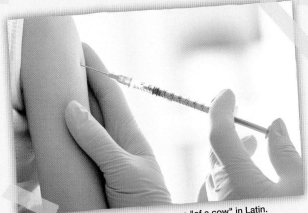

The word "vaccine" means "of a cow" in Latin.

Vaccination

Vaccines are weak versions of harmful microbes. They are given by injection to protect us from infectious diseases. Our bodies then produce antibodies, which are chemicals in the blood that fight infection. These antibodies stay in our blood, ready to attack the more harmful version if needed.

The first vaccine was developed in 1796 by English doctor Edward Jenner. He had noticed that women who worked milking cows did not catch the deadly disease smallpox if they had previously caught a milder disease called cowpox from cows. He injected people with the cowpox microbe and proved that it protected them against smallpox. Today, diseases such as smallpox and polio have been wiped out by vaccination.

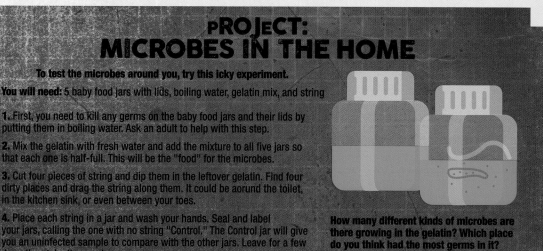

PROJECT:
MICROBES IN THE HOME

To test the microbes around you, try this icky experiment.

You will need: 5 baby food jars with lids, boiling water, gelatin mix, and string

1. First, you need to kill any germs on the baby food jars and their lids by putting them in boiling water. Ask an adult to help with this step.

2. Mix the gelatin with fresh water and add the mixture to all five jars so that each one is half-full. This will be the "food" for the microbes.

3. Cut four pieces of string and dip them in the leftover gelatin. Find four dirty places and drag the string along them. It could be aorund the toilet, in the kitchen sink, or even between your toes.

4. Place each string in a jar and wash your hands. Seal and label your jars, calling the one with no string "Control." The Control jar will give you an uninfected sample to compare with the other jars. Leave for a few days, then take them out.

How many different kinds of microbes are there growing in the gelatin? Which place do you think had the most germs in it?

EXPLAINING RADIATION

Radioactivity is a process by which the **atoms** of certain **elements** break up and give off energy. This energy is called radiation. Radiation was first discovered in 1896 by French scientist Henri Becquerel. It was French-Polish chemist Marie Curie who discovered how radiation is created.

Marie Curie (1867–1934)

Elements are the simplest chemical substances. Each element is made up of one kind of atom. Before the work of Marie Curie and her husband Pierre, scientists believed the atoms that make up the elements were the smallest units of matter possible. However, Curie showed that some atoms are unstable, which makes them break down into even smaller pieces. This process caused radiation. At the time, she did not know radiation could be dangerous. Sadly, her experiments eventually gave her a deadly form of cancer.

Unstable atoms

Curie worked with an element called uranium. It is made up of large, unstable atoms. We now know that the nuclei, or central cores, of atoms are made of smaller particles called protons and neutrons. Over time, uranium atoms decay, or break down, into smaller atoms of the element thorium. Thorium gives off radiation in the form of alpha particles made of two protons and two neutrons.

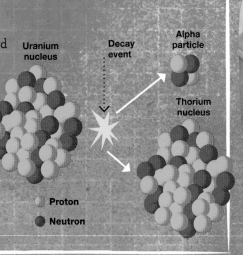

Uranium nucleus

Decay event

Alpha particle

Thorium nucleus

● Proton

● Neutron

Half-life

All radioactive material has a half-life, which is the length of time on average that it takes for half of the atoms to decay. However, it takes much longer for the material to totally decay. That means radioactive material can remain dangerous for a very long time. This is why waste from nuclear reactors, which make energy at nuclear power stations, must be securely sealed and stored for long periods.

Radiation protection

We are exposed to low levels of radiation every day, and it is harmless. However, exposure to high levels of radiation can cause deadly diseases. Some forms of radiation can be blocked very easily. Others require thick barriers.

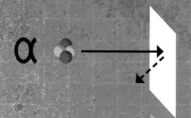

α

Alpha particles, such as those given off by atoms of uranium, can be blocked by a simple sheet of paper.

β

Beta particles, given off by atoms of tritium, can be blocked by a sheet of aluminium.

γ

Gamma particles, given off by atoms of radium, can only be blocked by a thick layer of lead.

PROJECT: HEADS OR TAILS?

To see how a half-life works over time, try this model using coins.

You will need: a resealable bag and about 120 coins

1. Count out exactly 100 coins and place them in the bag.

2. Shake the bag and carefully empty the coins onto a table.

3. Separate out the coins that are heads side up. Count them and write down the number. Place only these coins back in the bag.

4. Now repeat the process until there are no coins left.

To show a visual graph of your results, make piles of coins for each number you wrote down. What does your graph look like? Each turn represents one half-life of your stack. How many half-lives did it take to finish the project?

INHERITANCE AND GENETICS

It has been obvious to people for thousands of years that the traits of offspring are inherited, or passed on to them by their parents. However, before the work of Gregor Mendel, nobody knew how it happened.

Gregor Mendel
(1822–1884)

Austrian monk Mendel showed that the genes that control traits work in pairs. Each pair contains one gene inherited from each parent. This was the beginning of the science of genetics. Mendel experimented with pea plants he grew on the grounds of the monastery where he lived. The plants came in two varieties: one with purple flowers and one with white flowers.

Passing generations

Mendel crossbred purple-flower and white-flower plants to make mixed-breed **hybrids**. The first generation of hybrid plants all had purple flowers. But when these were crossbred with each other, Mendel found that white flowers appeared in a quarter of the second generation of plants.

Mendel suggested that flower color was controlled by one pair of genes, which could be either P, for purple, or W, for white. If a plant inherited two W genes from its parents, it had white flowers. But if a plant inherited two Ps or a P and a W, it had purple flowers. He described purple as being the dominant, or controlling, trait. He called white a recessive, or non-controlling, trait.

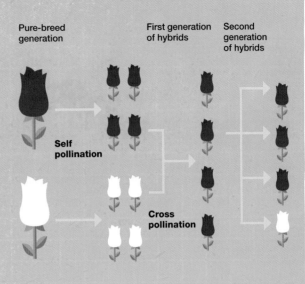

Pure-breed generation

First generation of hybrids

Second generation of hybrids

Self pollination

Cross pollination

Combining with Darwin

Mendel published his results in 1866, but they were ignored for several decades. His work was rediscovered in the 1900s. His ideas were combined with Charles Darwin's ideas (pages 10–11) to show how genes are the units of change in evolution.

These flowers are crocuses. Just like pea plants, their color is determined by their genes.

pROJeCT:
CAT TRAIT SURVEY

In cats, traits such as hair length and color are determined by single gene pairs. Investigate the genes of the cats in your neighborhood by carrying out a survey of the traits they display.

Create a table similar to the one below to conduct your survey. The hair-length gene can be labeled "L" or "l." The L will stand for short hair, and l will stand for long hair. L is the dominant gene and l is the recessive gene. Another gene determines whether hair is one solid color or is agouti hair, which has bands of different colors. Tabby cats have agouti hair. On your chart, use "A" for agouti, which is dominant. Use "a" for non-agouti, which is recessive. A third gene determines whether or not the cat has orange fur. The orange fur gene "O" is dominant, so any cat with one O gene will have some orange fur.

	Cat 1	Cat 2	Cat 3
Hair length	☐	☐	☐
Agouti	☐	☐	☐
Orange fur	☐	☐	☐

Using your table, can you determine which genes each cat in your neighborhood has? Is more than one combination possible?

LIGHT, SPACE, AND TIME

Few scientists can claim they have changed the way we view the universe, but this is exactly what German physicist Albert Einstein achieved with his Theory of **Relativity** in 1905.

Albert Einstein (1879–1955)

Einstein revolutionized physics with his theories, which he formulated while working as a clerk in a patent office in Switzerland. Einstein demonstrated that space and time form part of one structure called "space-time." He suggested when space-time is warped or curved by massive objects, other objects orbit or move along those curves, creating what we feel as the force of gravity.

Nuclear energy

Einstein's famous equation $E = mc^2$ shows that energy (E) is equal to mass (m) times the speed of light (c) squared—a very big number. This means that a small amount of mass can be converted into a huge amount of energy. For example, nuclear power stations create massive amounts of energy by splitting tiny atoms.

Einstein's famous equation explains why nuclear bombs create enormous explosions. A small amount of radioactive matter, such as plutonium, is turned into a huge amount of energy.

Gravitational lensing

Light travels in straight lines through space. However, when light passes near massive objects, it appears to curve due to the effect of the objects' gravity. This effect is called gravitational lensing. When the light of stars and **galaxies** passes close to another star on its way to us, the effect of gravity causes these stars and galaxies to appear to be in the wrong place when viewed from Earth.

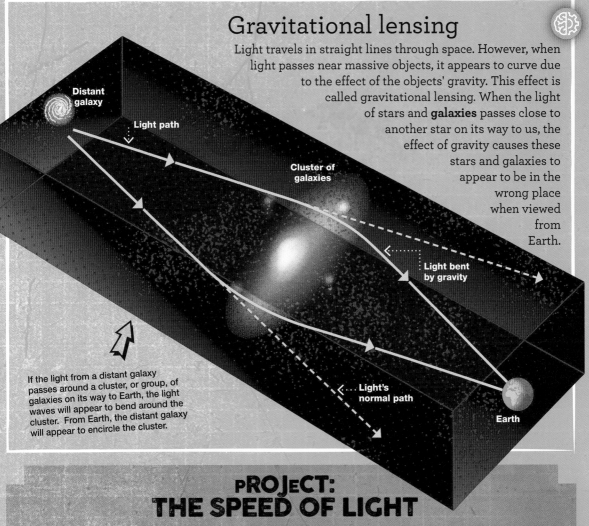

Distant galaxy

Light path

Cluster of galaxies

Light bent by gravity

Light's normal path

Earth

If the light from a distant galaxy passes around a cluster, or group, of galaxies on its way to Earth, the light waves will appear to bend around the cluster. From Earth, the distant galaxy will appear to encircle the cluster.

pROJeCT:
THE SPEED OF LIGHT

Light travels at a speed of about 186,000 miles (300,000 km) per second. According to relativity, nothing can travel faster, making this the "speed limit" of the universe. Microwaves travel at the same speed as light, so you can measure the speed of light using the waves in a microwave oven.

You will need: a microwave, four slices of bread, a microwaveable plate, margarine, and a calculator

1. Note the frequency of the microwave, which is marked on the oven. It should be marked as 2,450 MHz. (1 MHz is a frequency of 1,000,000 waves per second.)

2. Place four square slices of bread on a plate so that they are touching each other, and spread margarine thickly and evenly over the whole surface.

3. Remove the microwave's turntable, and place the plate on the base of the microwave in such a way that it will not rotate.

4. Close the door and run the microwave at full power for about 30 seconds. When melted patches start to appear, stop the microwave and take out the bread. Measure the distance between each patch as a fraction of feet or meters. Double this number to get the wavelength.

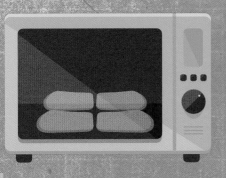

Time for some math: The frequency is the number of waves per second. The speed of the waves is equal to the wavelength multiplied by the frequency. A microwave oven has a frequency of 2,450 MHz, which means there are 2,450,000,000 waves per second. If the wavelength is 0.3 feet (0.09 m), then the speed is:
0.3 x 2,450,000,000 = 735,000,000 ft/s, or 139,205 miles/s
(0.09 x 2,450,000,000 = 220,500,000 m/s, or 220,500 km)
What is your number?

AN EXPANDING UNIVERSE

In the 1920s, American astronomer Edwin Hubble demonstrated that our universe is vastly bigger than most people had previously thought. He also showed that it is getting even bigger.

Edwin Hubble
(1889–1953)

After many nights of careful observation through a telescope, Hubble showed that faint objects in the sky, called nebulae, were actually distant galaxies far beyond our own Milky Way galaxy. He observed that most of these galaxies were moving away from us, and that the farther away they were, the faster they were moving. This was evidence that the universe is expanding.

There are more than 100 billion galaxies in the universe.

The Doppler effect

Hubble measured the speed at which the galaxies were moving using a phenomenon called the Doppler effect. This effect states that a wavelength of light becomes longer if an object is moving away from us. This is known as redshift. The greater the redshift, the faster the movement.

The Doppler effect also affects sound waves. For example, the noise from an ambulance siren changes between high and low pitch as the vehicle passes us. As the ambulance approaches us, it starts to catch up with its own sound waves. This means the waves bunch up, producing shorter waves and a higher pitch. As it moves away, the waves become longer, making the pitch lower.

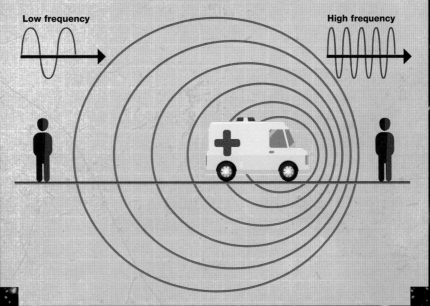

Low frequency

High frequency

pROJeCT:
INFLATING SPACE

As the universe expands, objects that are the farthest away appear to move the fastest apart. This experiment shows why that is.

You will need: a balloon, a marker, and a ruler

1. Inflate the balloon slightly, then draw five dots on the balloon in a straight line, about 1 inch (2.5 cm) apart. Imagine that the surface of the balloon is your universe.

2. Now blow up the balloon as far as it will go and measure the distance between the dots.

The farther the dots are from one another at the start, the faster they will travel as the balloon is inflated. Try it again with the dots farther apart at the start. How much faster did the dots travel this time?

THE START OF THE UNIVERSE

The Belgian priest and physicist Georges Lemaître built on the work of Edwin Hubble to produce an entirely new theory for the start of the universe.

Georges Lemaître (1894–1966)

Since the universe is expanding, Lemaître reasoned that it must have been smaller in the past. Working backward through time, he proposed that the universe had begun at a particular moment as just a tiny atom.

First atomic nuclei appear after three minutes

Stars appear after 200 million years

Big Bang

First atoms form after 400,000 years

The latest measurements estimate that the Big Bang took place 13.81 billion years ago.

Proving the theory

Lemaître published his idea in 1931, and it proved to be highly controversial. Dismissing the theory, the English astronomer Fred Hoyle described it mockingly as a "Big Bang" theory. The name stuck, and it wasn't until the 1960s that more evidence was found to support his theory. The theory states that the universe should be filled with microwave radiation, first released when the universe was 300,000 years old. Known as the the Cosmic Microwave Background (CMB), this radiation was first detected in 1964. An image of it is shown on the right. It appeared to be just as Lemaître's theory had predicted.

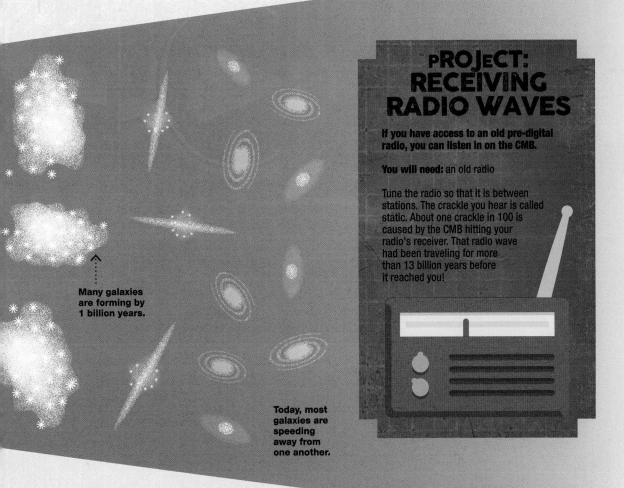

Many galaxies are forming by 1 billion years.

Today, most galaxies are speeding away from one another.

pROJECT: RECEIVING RADIO WAVES

If you have access to an old pre-digital radio, you can listen in on the CMB.

You will need: an old radio

Tune the radio so that it is between stations. The crackle you hear is called static. About one crackle in 100 is caused by the CMB hitting your radio's receiver. That radio wave had been traveling for more than 13 billion years before it reached you!

THE RESHAPING OF EARTH

Earth's hard top layer, called the crust, is made up of several large pieces of land, which float on **magma**. German scientist Alfred Wegener called them tectonic plates. These plates move 1 to 2 inches (3 to 5 cm) every year. This process, called continental drift, slowly reshapes Earth's surface.

Alfred Wegener (1880–1930)

The theory of continental drift was first proposed by Alfred Wegener in 1912. Wegener's idea explained why similar fossils can be found on different continents. However, most **geologists** refused to believe that such movement was possible. In the 1950s, accurate measurements were able to show that large sections of Earth's crust were indeed moving. Wegener's theory was finally accepted more than 20 years after his death.

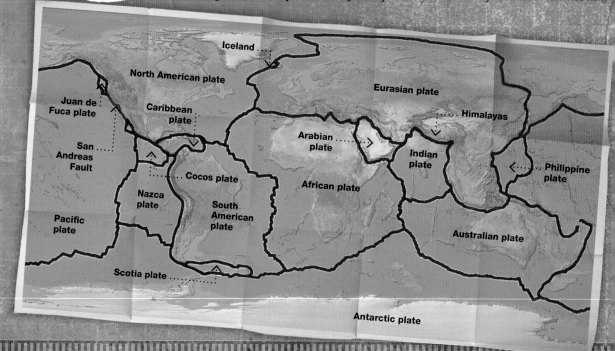

- Iceland
- North American plate
- Juan de Fuca plate
- Caribbean plate
- San Andreas Fault
- Cocos plate
- Nazca plate
- Pacific plate
- South American plate
- Scotia plate
- African plate
- Arabian plate
- Eurasian plate
- Himalayas
- Indian plate
- Philippine plate
- Australian plate
- Antarctic plate

Convergent boundary

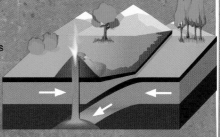

Changes to Earth's surface happen in different ways. Here, plates are converging, or moving toward one another. One plate moves beneath the other. Mountain ranges can form at convergent boundaries. The Himalayas formed when the Indian and Asian plates converged 50 million years ago. The mountains are still growing about half an inch (1 cm) every year.

Divergent boundary

When plates are divergent, they are moving away from one another. The space is filled by molten rock beneath the crust, which cools to form new crust. This results in frequent activity from volcanoes. Divergent boundaries are often found under the oceans and on volcanic islands such as Iceland.

Transform boundary

With a transform boundary, plates slide past one another. Pressure between the plates builds up over time and is released abruptly as they shift position, causing violent earthquakes. Movement at a transform boundary in California, called the San Andreas Fault, caused an earthquake in 1906 that destroyed much of San Francisco.

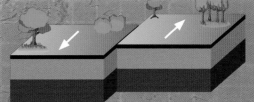

Pangaea

225 million years ago (mya)

150 mya

65 mya

Today

Around 200 million years ago, all of Earth's continents were joined together into one super-continent known as Pangaea. Since the planet formed more than 4.5 billion years ago, it is believed that there have been several different supercontinents, each of which eventually broke apart. There is evidence to show that today's continents are slowly moving toward each other. In the future, the continents may join again and form a new supercontinent.

PROJECT: MOVING PLATES

Create a map of tectonic plates on a large piece of cardboard.

You will need:
1 cup (237 ml) salt, 2 cups (473 ml) flour, 3/4 cup (177 ml) water, a spatula, two bowls, cardboard, and red and brown food coloring

1. Draw tectonic plates on the cardboard. Use the map on page 24 as a guide. Draw the plates at different distances from one another, some nearly touching, others a little apart. Then combine the salt and flour in a bowl and slowly add water. Mix to form a thick paste.

2. Separate the paste into two bowls. Add red food coloring to one and brown food coloring to the other. Spread brown mixture on the plates and smooth it with the spatula.

3. Add red mixture into spaces between plates—this represents magma oozing between the cracks where the plates are separating.

Dry your salt map overnight, and label the plates the next day.

THE GENETIC CODE FOR LIFE

In the early 1900s, scientists discovered that genes inside the **cells** of living things are contained in **molecules** called **chromosomes**. Made of strands of a substance called deoxyribonucleic acid (DNA), chromosomes form the **genetic code** for life. By the 1950s, the race was on to discover how DNA molecules were made.

Rosalind Franklin (1920–1958)

English **biophysicist** Rosalind Franklin made the first breakthrough in the discovery of the structure of DNA. She died very young, and her contribution to science was only fully recognized after her death.

Every DNA molecule is shaped like a twisted ladder called a double-helix. The rungs of the ladders are made up pairs of genetic materials that control characteristics that are inherited.

The key breakthrough

In 1953, Rosalind Franklin took an X-ray of DNA that showed an X-like structure. Franklin's colleagues James Watson and Francis Crick realized that some parts of the image were not visible, and the shape was actually a double-helix, which is a pair of spiral strands. They figured out that DNA was made up of pairs of genes connected to one another in the middle, as well as to the strands of the helix, like rungs on a ladder.

Base pairs

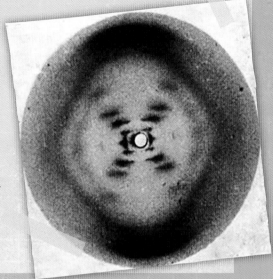

Cracking the code

Once the structure of DNA was known, scientists began the long process of figuring out the full DNA code. The entire **sequence** of genes is called the genome. Each species has a different one. In 2003, the Human Genome Project sequenced the entire human genome, consisting of more than 20,000 genes. This paves the way for new treatments to be developed called gene therapy. In the future, doctors hope to be able to just replace defective genes instead of having to use drugs or surgery to prevent or cure diseases.

pROJeCT:
THE DNA TEST

The genomes of many different animals have now been sequenced and are listed on the website www.genomesize.com. The size of the genome is given by a number called its "C value." The larger the C value, the bigger the genome.

You will need: a computer with Internet access

Look through the genome website's online database (see address above) and compare the C values of different kinds of animals. Choose animals that you think are very different from one another and make a list of their C values.

Are the results as you expected? Scientists have been surprised to find that some very simple animals have a lot of DNA, while some more complex ones have much less. An amoeba, which is an animal with a single cell, can have 100 times more DNA than humans!

THE ORIGIN OF CELLS

The billions of cells in our bodies are complex structures with many internal parts. One part in the center, called the nucleus, contains our DNA. Other parts called mitochondria are the "power packs" of cells, which release the energy needed for life. These complex cells have evolved, or changed over time, in a process called symbiosis. Symbiosis is a relationship where different **organisms** live together and provide each other with benefits.

Lynn Margulis
(1938–2011)

American **biologist** Lynn Margulis first proposed the theory that all complex life could have started through symbiosis. She theorized that hundreds of millions of years ago, complex cells first formed when small bacteria-like cells were eaten by larger cells. Instead of dying, the cells thrived inside the larger cells, becoming the mitochondria that give cells a boost of energy. Margulis's theory is widely accepted today.

pROJeCT:
SYMBIOSIS IN ACTION

There are many examples of symbiosis all around us. To see how plants rely on bacteria to help them grow, try this project.

You will need: six identical pots, sterilized potting soil, pea seeds, inoculating loop, Rhizobium Leguminosarum culture (bacteria available from garden centers)

1. Label three pots "Control" and three pots "Bacteria." Using exactly the same amount of soil in the pots, plant three seeds in each one and place them in a sunny place. Remember to water them regularly.

2. After five days, use the inoculating loop to add half a teaspoon (2.5 ml) of bacteria to each of the pots marked "Bacteria." Leave the plants to grow for nine weeks and record their progress.

What difference did the bacteria make?

CONTROL

Inoculating loop

A cross section
of a human cell

Nucleus

Mitochondrion

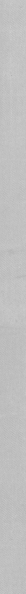

GLOSSARY

ASTRONOMER A scientist who studies space and the universe

ATOMS The smallest particles of a chemical element

BIOLOGIST A scientist who studies organisms and living things of all kinds

BIOPHYSICIST A scientist who applies the study of matter and energy to living things

CELL Building block of living organisms.

CHEMIST A scientist who studies matter and its properties

CHROMOSOMES Thread-like structures found in cells, each made of a single molecule of DNA

ELEMENTS Substances that are each made from just one kind of atom

FORCE A push or pull on an object

GALAXIES Massive collections of stars

GENES Sections of a chromosome that control the traits an organism will have

GENETIC CODE The set of rules living cells use to encode and decode hereditary information

GEOLOGISTS Scientists who study Earth and its processes

HYBRIDS Animals or plants that have parents of two different varieties

MAGMA The layer of hot rock beneath Earth's crust

MASS The amount of matter contained in an object

MICROBES Organisms so small they can only be seen through a microscope

MICROWAVES Waves of electro-magnetic radiation that can heat food or carry communications signals

MOLECULES The smallest particle of a substance, made from two or more atoms

NATURALIST A person who studies nature, especially plants or animals

ORGANISMS Individual life-forms, such as an animal, a plant, or a bacterium

PHYSICIST A scientist that studies matter and energy, and how they act

PRISM A transparent object that usually has three sides and can bend light

REFRACTION The bending of light passing from one substance to another

RELATIVITY The theory that states the speed of light is constant, and all other elements, such as time, space, and mass, change depending on how fast the viewer is moving through space

REPRODUCTION The process by which organisms produce offspring

SEQUENCE To determine the chemical code that makes up every single rung of DNA in each human chromosome

SUBATOMIC PARTICLES The smaller units from which atoms are made

THEORIES Ideas that are the starting points for argument or investigation

TRAIT A feature of an organism that is determined by the organism's genes

VELOCITY The speed of an object and its direction of travel

p. 7 Camera obscura

The image is upside-down. The hole in the camera obscura acts like the pupil in an eye.

p. 9 Ball and ramps

The distance traveled is proportional to a square of the time. When you double the time the ball has rolled, it traveled four times as far.

p. 13 Microbes in the home

You may find colonies of different kinds of bacteria and fungi growing in your jars. The places with the most microbes will vary, but your body is likely to have more microbes than most other places.

p. 15 Heads or tails?

On average, it will take between seven and ten half-lives before you run out of coins. One half-life of a radioactive material can vary from a fraction of a second to billions of years. But it will take many more half-lives for all the material to decay.

p. 17 Cat trait survey

If a cat has a recessive trait such as long hair, this shows it must have two of the same genes: in this case, l–l. However, if a cat has a dominant trait such as short hair, there are two possible gene combinations: in this case, Ll or LL.

31

p. 21 Inflating space

At the start, the dots were approximately 1 inch (2.5 cm) apart. At the end, they might be 2 inches (5 cm) apart, meaning the distance they traveled was 1 inch (2.5 cm). If the dots were 3 inches (7.5 cm) apart at the start, they might be 6 inches (15 cm) from one another at the end, meaning they traveled a distance of 3 inches (7.5 cm). That's three times the distance in the same time, so they were moving three times faster.

p. 29 Symbiosis in action

The plants with bacteria will be bigger and stronger than the plants without bacteria. The bacteria help the plant to take nitrogen from the air, which is essential for growth.

INDEX